CW01390773

30109 05355657 0

THE
HUNGRY
HISTORY OF
SHARKS

W

FRANKLIN WATTS

LONDON • SYDNEY

Clive Gifford and
Andressa Meissner

First published in Great Britain in 2024 by Hodder and Stoughton

Text and design © Hodder and Stoughton, 2024

Illustrations © Andressa Meissner 2024.

All rights reserved

Managing editor: Victoria Brooker / Design: Gemma Steward

ISBN: 9781445190525 (hbk) / ISBN: 9781445190549 (pbk) / ISBN: 9781445190532 (ebk)

Franklin Watts, an imprint of Hachette Children's Group
Part of Hodder and Stoughton
Carmelite House, 50 Victoria Embankment, London EC4Y 0DZ

An Hachette UK Company

www.hachette.co.uk
www.hachettechildrens.co.uk

Printed and bound in Dubai

MIX
Paper | Supporting
responsible forestry
FSC® C104740

CONTENTS

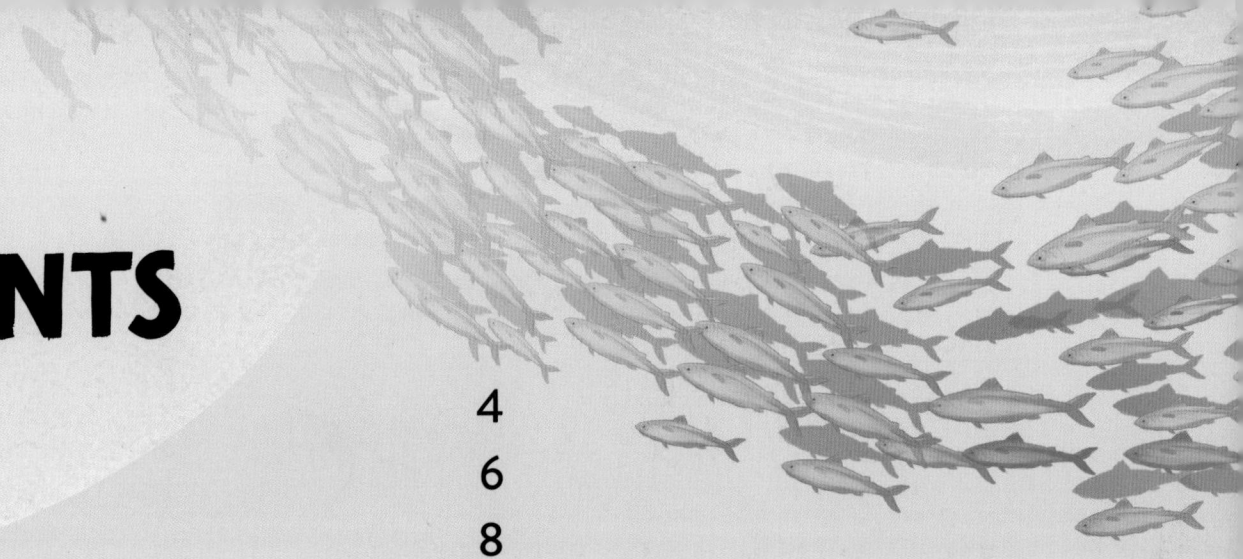

A WORLD OF SHARKS

THINK ALL SHARKS ARE MAN—EATING TERRORS? THINK AGAIN!
THERE'S SO MUCH MORE TO THESE FASCINATING, OFTEN
PEACEFUL AND FREQUENTLY MISUNDERSTOOD, CREATURES.

Sharks are amongst the most successful and ancient of
all sea dwellers. Some can surprise with their amazing
attributes like the sandbar shark which can go through
35,000 teeth in its lifetime or the Greenland shark
which can live to be 400 years old.

Tiger shark

Panama catshark

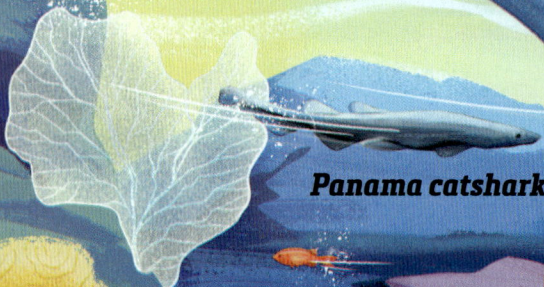

Great Whites, Tiger and Hammerheads may be the
most famous, but sharks vary far more than you
think. There are some 544 species. These range in
size from whale sharks longer than buses to Panama
catsharks and dwarf lantern sharks which could sit
across the palm of your hand.

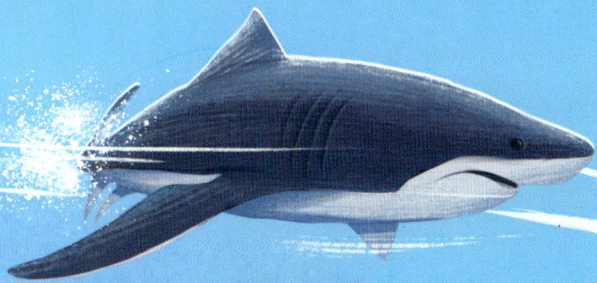

Great white shark

Some sharks feed on microscopic plankton, others hunt seals, dolphins and whales.

Hammerhead shark

The bonnethead shark chomps down on seagrass, in between dining on blue crabs. It's one of the few plant-eating sharks.

Bonnethead shark

This book takes you through the hungry history of these incredible creatures.

5

SHARK RELATIVES

Sharks join rays, skates and sawfish in a class of more than 1,000 different creatures called Chondrichthyes. All these species are known as cartilaginous fishes as they have a flexible skeleton made of gristly cartilage instead of bone.

Mobula ray

Most rays live on or close to the sea bed but mobula rays sometimes take to the air. They leap spectacularly out of the water and belly flop their diamond-shaped bodies on landing – an amazing sight.

Oceanic manta ray

The largest ray of all is the oceanic manta ray. These big beasts can grow up to 8.5 m wide and feed on tiny plankton in the ocean water. Flaps called cephalic lobes help funnel water and food into their mouths.

Clearnose skate

Skates are closely related to rays but differ because they lay eggs. There are over 150 species. The clearnose skate lives in muddy sea floors where it hunts shellfish, shrimp, crabs and small fish, mainly at night.

SAWFISH

Each of the five species of sawfish has a long, bladed snout called a rostrum. It is covered in teeth and looks a little like a garden hedgetrimmer! The rostrum is used both to defend itself and to hunt prey – mostly crustaceans and small fish. It contains organs which detect electrical signals given off by other creatures (see pages 18-19).

Largetooth sawfish

The largetooth sawfish grows up to 7 m long and spends the first years of its life living in freshwater rivers before moving out to sea.

PREHISTORIC SHARKS

Many creatures come and go, but sharks have been around for hundreds of millions of years. Early ancestors of modern sharks were swimming the prehistoric seas more than 150 million years before the first dinosaurs arrived.

CLADOSELACHE

Scientists think that around 420 million years ago, different cartilaginous fish groups diverged, which led to the first shark-like creatures evolving. Within 40 million years, distant ancestors of today's sharks, like the 2-m-long, torpedo-shaped Cladoselache, could be found living in the oceans.

HELICOPRION

Early sharks had small jaws at the end of their snouts, but some species began evolving with monstrous mouths. Helicoprion arrived around 290 million years ago. Its teeth were arranged in a spiral pattern bigger than a dinner plate. They looked like a circular saw.

EDESTUS

Around 200 million years ago, some sharks evolved with large, flexible jaws that allowed them to bite and swallow large prey. Edestus had curving jaws with teeth that stuck out at odd angles.

STETHACANTHUS

Other strange adaptations also occurred. Stethacanthus had a head covered in small spikes and a large fin on its back shaped like an anvil. We don't know for certain what its purpose was.

XENACANTHUS

Some sharks, like the eel-shaped Xenacanthus, could be found in prehistoric rivers and swamps. It had a large, possibly venomous, spike sticking out of its head and unusual V-shaped teeth.

THE MEG

The largest known shark lived between 20 million and 2.6 million years ago. When fossils were first discovered of Otodus megalodon, people couldn't quite believe its epic scale. 'The Meg', as it has become nicknamed, would have grown to around three times the size of the biggest shark today – the Great White.

Megalodon lived throughout the prehistoric oceans. Fossils of this huge beast have been found on all the world's continents except Antarctica. Experts estimate that adult females were larger than males, growing up to 16- to 18-m-long and weighing as much as 61 tonnes – the weight of ten African elephants.

A shark of this gargantuan size may have needed a whopping 98,000 calories of food a day. That is equal to consuming more than one tonne of fish of flesh every day. We think it hunted dolphins, whales and other sharks. It may have eaten creatures up to the size of a modern great white shark (see pages 36-37).

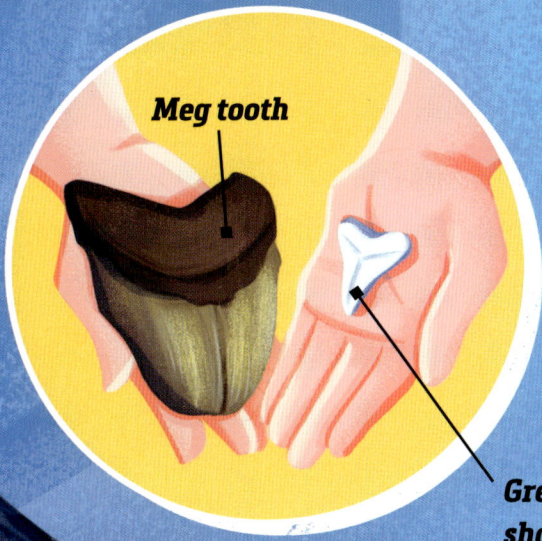

Meg tooth

Great white shark tooth

Megalodon means 'giant teeth' and the creature's jaws were lined with at least 270 sharp, triangular teeth. Some grew as large as 18 cm and could easily span the width of a human hand.

A formidable hunter, the Meg possessed a truly huge jaw, up to 3.4 m across and opening wide enough to be capable of swallowing three or four people at the same time. It could probably eat whole whales in just a few bites. Powerful jaw muscles would have created an immense bite force perhaps 8-10 times as powerful as a great white's. As megalodon clamped its jaws down on prey, its bite would shear through bone or crush it.

SHARK PARTS

Whilst sharks vary greatly in shape and size, they share many crucial features. These tiger sharks are large predators that typically grow to 3.25–4.5 m long. They eat almost anything, from turtles, lobsters and sea birds to porpoises, rays and other sharks.

The wedge-shaped head can be quickly moved through water, allowing the shark to turn quickly.

Its powerful, torpedo-shaped body is packed with muscle.

Nostril

Gill slits are openings which let water pass over the gills where oxygen is absorbed into the shark's blood.

Long pectoral fins act as wings underwater, giving the shark lift. They can be raised and lowered independently to help the creature steer.

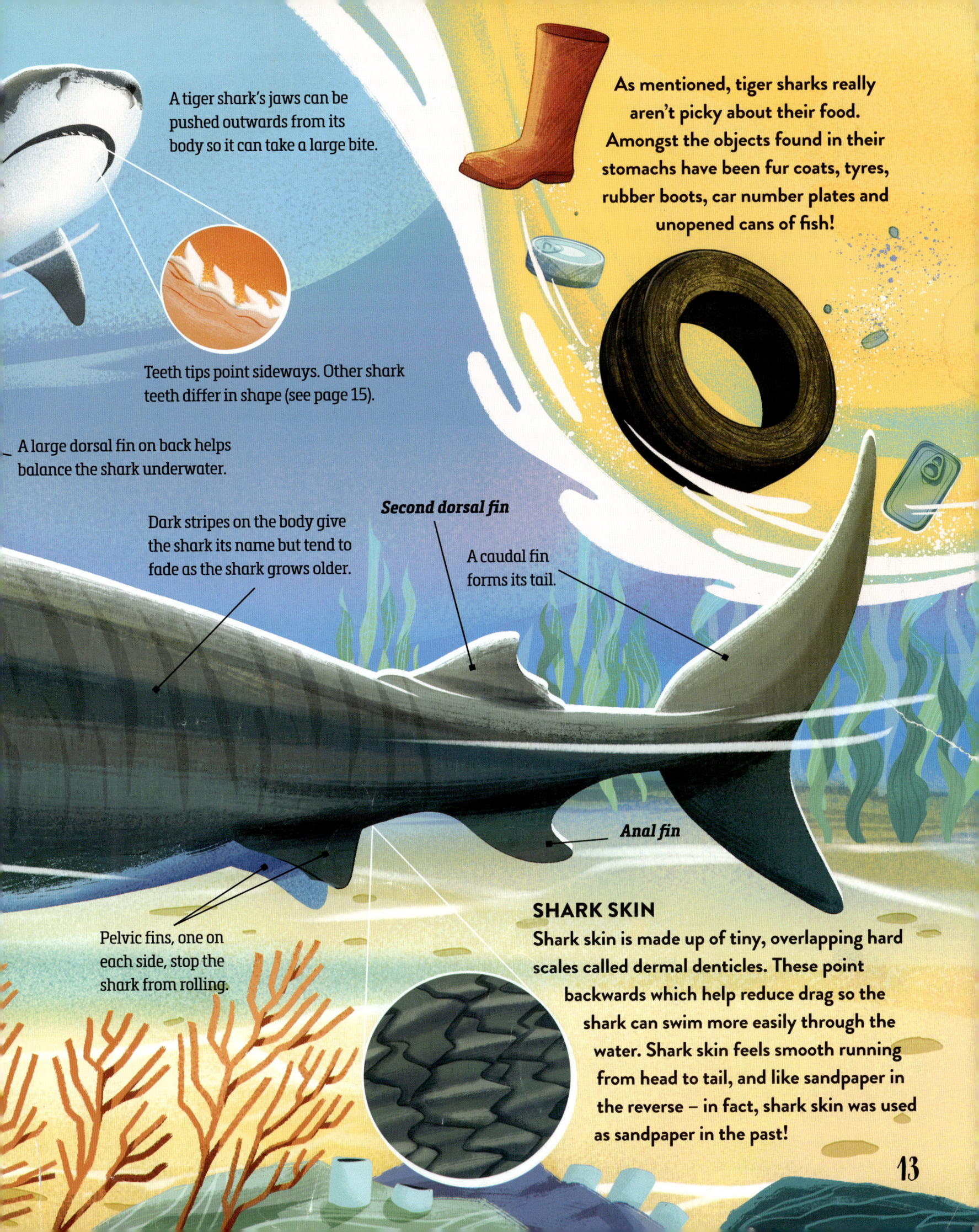

A tiger shark's jaws can be pushed outwards from its body so it can take a large bite.

Teeth tips point sideways. Other shark teeth differ in shape (see page 15).

A large dorsal fin on back helps balance the shark underwater.

Dark stripes on the body give the shark its name but tend to fade as the shark grows older.

Second dorsal fin

A caudal fin forms its tail.

As mentioned, tiger sharks really aren't picky about their food. Amongst the objects found in their stomachs have been fur coats, tyres, rubber boots, car number plates and unopened cans of fish!

Pelvic fins, one on each side, stop the shark from rolling.

Anal fin

SHARK SKIN

Shark skin is made up of tiny, overlapping hard scales called dermal denticles. These point backwards which help reduce drag so the shark can swim more easily through the water. Shark skin feels smooth running from head to tail, and like sandpaper in the reverse – in fact, shark skin was used as sandpaper in the past!

13

INSIDE A SHARK

From their skeleton made of materials lighter than bone to their large brains and giant livers, sharks are adapted perfectly for their lives underwater.

Backbone
Made of stiff cartilage, this supports the other parts of the shark's skeleton and protects the spinal cord.

Tail
This consists of a cartilage frame and strong muscles. Many sharks rely on powerful tail movements to propel themselves quickly through the water.

Stomach
Made of extremely stretchy muscle, this can expand greatly when the shark eats a large meal.

Sharks can invert their stomach to push it out of their mouths and clean it in seawater. They do this to get rid of waste they cannot digest, such as large bones.

Intestine

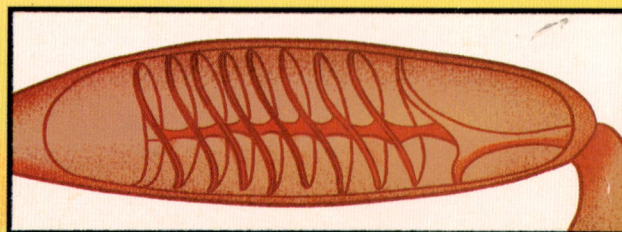

Spiral valve
This increases the surface area of the intestine, allowing more nutrients from food to be absorbed into the shark's blood.

THE WHOLE TOOTH

Shark teeth vary per species – from long, thin, pointed needles good for spearing small fish to heavy flat teeth suitable for cracking shells. Sharks have many rows of teeth with the biggest at the front and those still growing in the back rows. They replace their teeth constantly – some sharks go through more than 20,000 teeth during their lifetime.

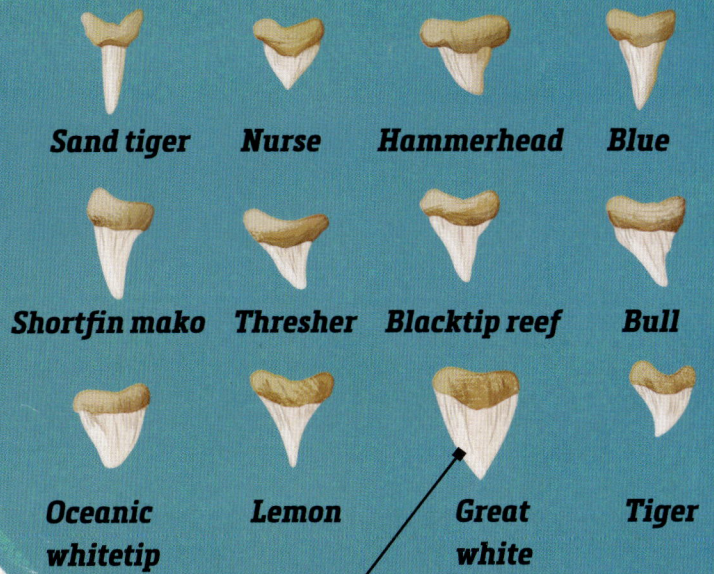

Sand tiger

Nurse

Hammerhead

Blue

Shortfin mako

Thresher

Blacktip reef

Bull

Oceanic whitetip

Lemon

Great white

Tiger

Large hunters, like the great white, have stout, triangular teeth with a serrated edge like a saw, perfect for biting and tearing flesh.

Muscle
Stout bands of muscle make most sharks strong swimmers. Sharks have two types of muscle: red which allows sharks to swim for a long time, and white which gives them short, powerful bursts of movement.

Muscle layers

Brain

Kidney

Gill arch
Gill arches are part of the skeleton.

Gill slits

Heart

Gill rakers
Gill rakers help keep food from flowing out of the gills.

Liver
This large organ is full of low density oil. It helps the shark stay neutrally buoyant, meaning it neither rises or sinks in the water. The basking shark's gigantic liver makes up a quarter of its body weight.

Gills
Oxygen from water is absorbed by blood vessels when the water passes over the shark's gills. The water exits the shark through openings called gill slits.

15

BABY SHARKS

THE MAJORITY OF SHARKS AND RAYS (ABOUT THREE-FIFTHS) ARE VIVIPAROUS – THEY ARE BORN AS LIVE YOUNG. SOME THOUGH, ARE OVIPAROUS – THEY HATCH OUT OF EGGS WHICH ARE LAID IN THE SEA.

Great white sharks are viviparous and mothers bear litters of between two and ten shark pups. Hammerhead sharks litters contain 20-40 pups whilst blue sharks sometimes birth litters of more than 100 pups, but not all of them survive.

Baby sand tiger shark

Sand tiger shark

The sand tiger shark develops many eggs and embryos inside the mother's body but only one or two live sharks will be born. The first to hatch and grow strong eats up all of its potential brothers and sisters whilst still inside its mother.

Lemon sharks are absent parents. They give birth in shallow waters containing mangrove forests for shelter and swim away, leaving the pups to fend for themselves. Surviving pups don't leave the safety of the mangroves for 3-7 years and females will return to the exact place they were born many years later to give birth to their own litters of pups.

Carpet sharks (see page 30) and horn sharks lay eggs, as does the curious Port Jackson shark found off the coast of Australia. The females produce large egg cases shaped like a corkscrew and almost the size of the mother shark's head.

They are carried in the mother's mouth and are sometimes wedged into sand or gaps between rocks for safety.

MERMAID'S PURSE

This is the nickname given to the leathery case that protects one or more shark (or ray) eggs. Some cases have long tendrils which snag on rocks or seaweed so that they don't drift away.

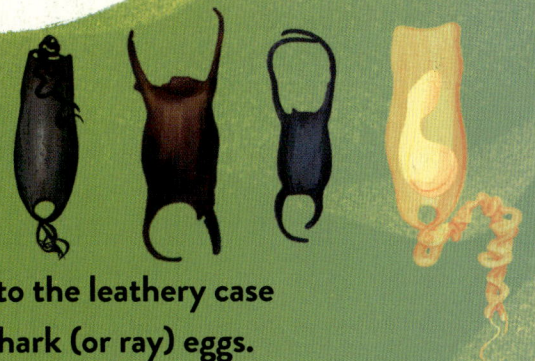

SHARK SENSES

Sharks are successful marine creatures partly because of the toolkit of super senses they possess. Whilst most sharks have a less developed sense of taste, their other senses are incredibly sharp and impressive.

SIGHT

Some deepwater sharks rely less on eyesight and more on other senses, but many sharks have sharp eyesight, especially over shorter distances. Some have third eyelids called nictitating membranes. These act as safety goggles, covering the eyes as the shark hunts, battles and feeds.

The bigeye thresher shark is well-named – its eyeball can be 10 cm wide, bigger than a softball.

GOOD VIBRATIONS

Sharks have fluid-filled canals called lateral lines running the length of their body. Small pores (holes) let seawater into the canals where sensory cells called neuromasts detect vibrations in the water. This allows the shark to detect the direction and amount of movement of other creatures many metres away, even if they cannot see them.

SMELL

Sharks have an incredibly accurate sense of smell – as good as sniffing out a single drop of blood in an entire swimming pool. A shark's nostrils can detect smells independently, like your ears detect sounds, so can work out the direction of a smell's source.

HEARING

Small holes above the shark's eyes lead to internal ears. Sound travels 4 ½ times faster through water than air so it is often the first sense sharks use to detect potential prey. Sharks focus on low rhythmical sounds given out by wounded or ill creatures in distress.

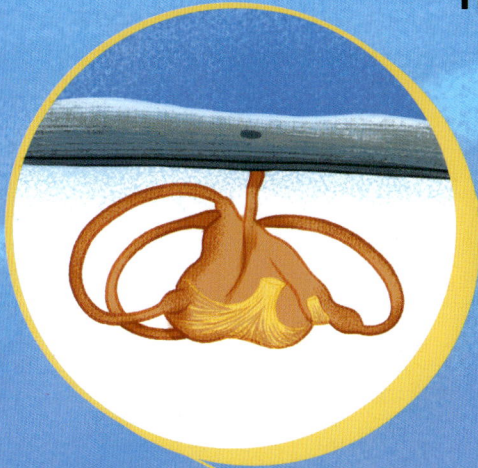

Some sharks can hear sounds more than 1 km away.

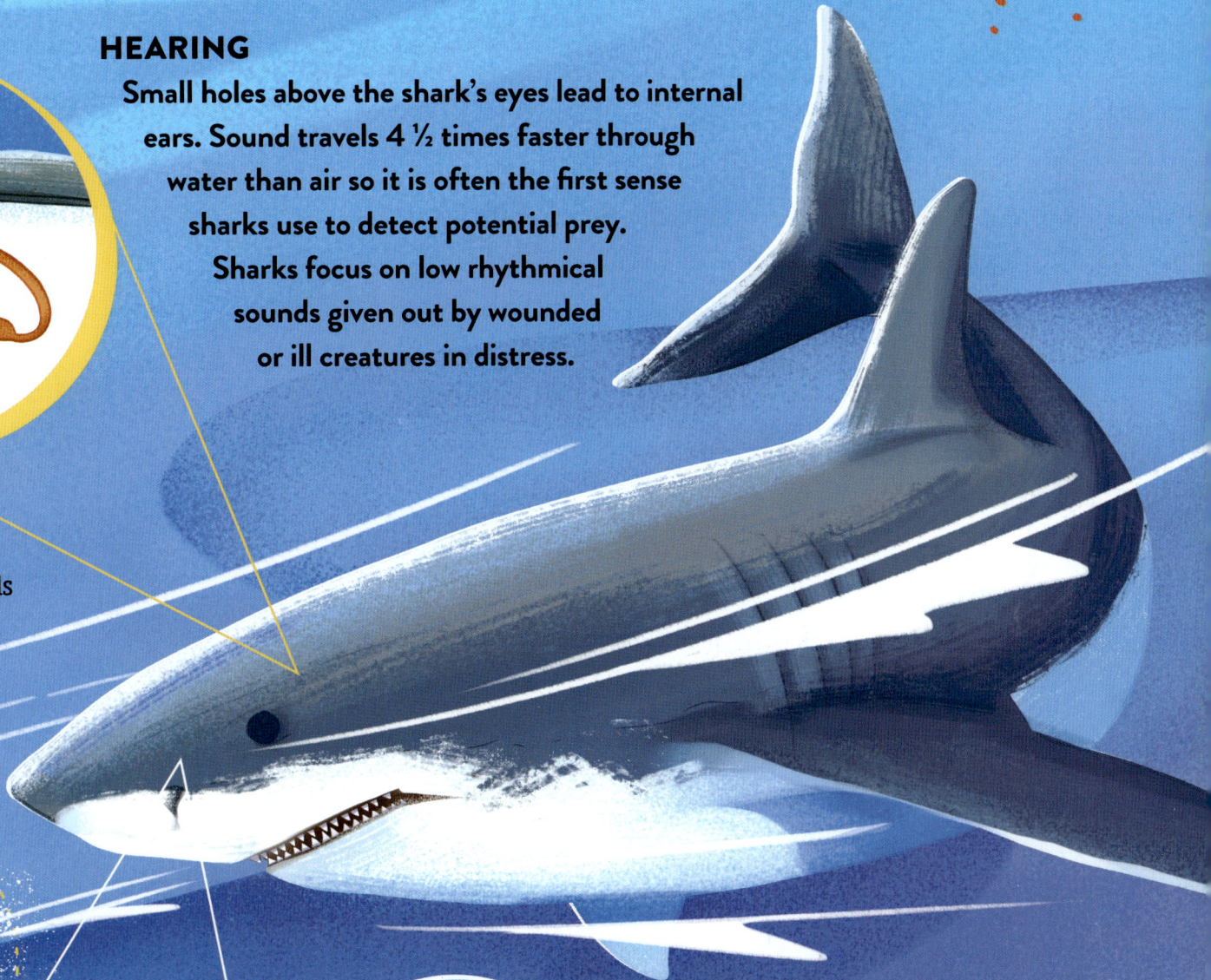

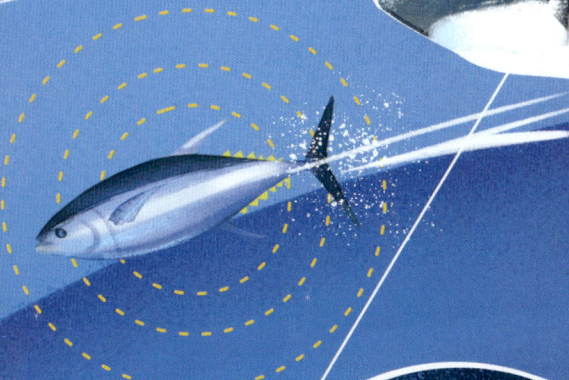

ampullae of Lorenzini

ELECTRIC DETECTOR

Sharks' snouts are covered in tiny pits full of jelly called ampullae of Lorenzini. These pick up weak electrical signals given out by the muscles, like a heartbeat, of other creatures in the water.

19

ON THE HUNT

Sharks don't all hunt in the same way. Some species, such as angel sharks (see pages 26–27, like to ambush using cunning and lightning reactions. Other sharks have evolved different ways of targeting and catching prey.

TAIL WEAPON

The top part of a 3-m-long pelagic thresher shark's tail fin is huge – as long as its entire body. The shark can flick its tail round at speed like a whip to strike and stun fish such as mackerel and small tuna, before going in for the kill.

AERIAL ATTACK

Some great whites accelerate to the sea's surface and launch themselves out of the water to catch fast-moving prey like seals. This is called a 'polaris breach' and is only used occasionally as it uses up a lot of the shark's energy and is only successful half the time.

PACK HUNTING

Bronze whaler sharks (also known as copper sharks) have been spotted working together in hunting packs off the coast of South Africa. There, they cooperate to herd thousands of sardines together into a tight ball. They then take turns to race through the densely packed fish with their large mouths wide open to feed greedily.

SPEEDY SHARK

The shortfin mako is warmer-blooded than most sharks. Its body temperature can be up to 6°C higher than the surrounding water. This helps give it the energy to swim rapidly – up to 70 km/h in short bursts. At such speeds, even fast fish like tuna and swordfish rarely escape.

BULL SHARKS

Unusually, these sharks can live in salt water and freshwater, weeing 20 times more when living in freshwater to keep the balance of chemicals in their body healthy.

They spend the first 5-7 years of their life in rivers before heading out to sea where they hunt mostly in shallow waters.

2.4 – 3.8 m

Bull sharks average 2.4–3.8 m long, have a stocky build and a particularly strong bite courtesy of their powerful jaw muscles.

Bull sharks mostly feed on bony fishes, stingrays and other sharks, including their own species. They are one of the few sharks known occasionally to bite humans unprovoked.

BLUE SHARKS

These beautiful sharks are a dazzling, almost metallic, blue colour on top and white on the bottom. This is called countershading and acts as camouflage, allowing the shark to sneak up on prey unseen from above or below.

3 m

A typical blue shark is just over 3 metres long and has a slender body. They can swim fast in short bursts when hunting.

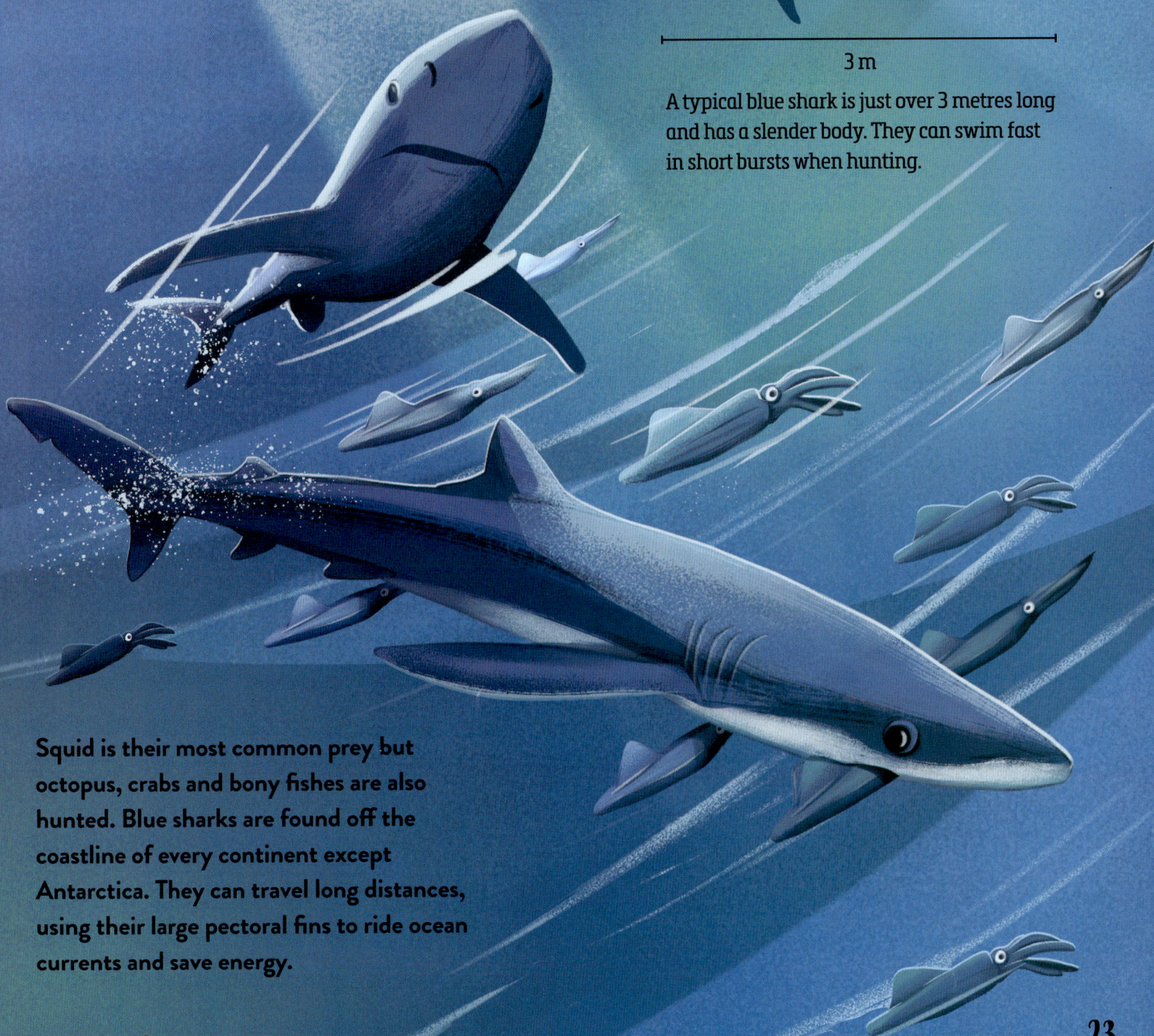

Squid is their most common prey but octopus, crabs and bony fishes are also hunted. Blue sharks are found off the coastline of every continent except Antarctica. They can travel long distances, using their large pectoral fins to ride ocean currents and save energy.

23

REEF SHARKS

THE WORLD'S CORAL REEFS PROVIDE RICH HABITATS FOR LARGE AMOUNTS OF MARINE LIFE AND THAT INCLUDES SHARKS. SHARKS ARE USUALLY A CORAL REEF'S APEX PREDATORS — AT THE TOP OF A REEF'S FOOD CHAIN.

Sharks help keep a reef ecosystem balanced by consuming some of the larger predatory fish, like groupers, that hunt smaller reef fish. Sharks can be messy eaters, meaning scraps of their prey drift away, providing food for other creatures.

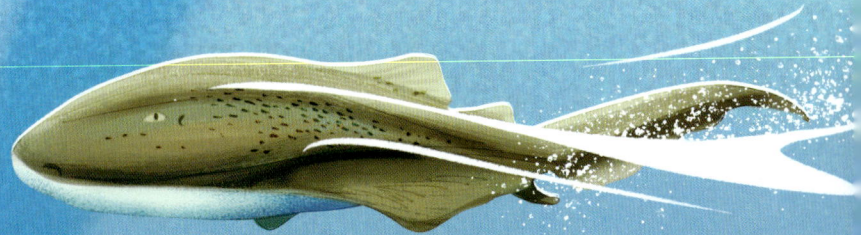

Leopard shark

Leopard sharks prefer shallow waters in and around reefs. They tend to dwell near the sea bed where they eat clams, crabs, shrimp and smaller tropical fish.

A coral reef provides sheltered places for smaller sharks to hide or be a nursery where baby sharks can develop and grow.

Grey reef sharks specialise in hunting reef fish that are less than 30 cm long. They are strong, agile swimmers, able to twist and turn to chase down their prey. They are active during both the day and night.

Grey reef shark

When threatened, some grey reef sharks raise their snouts, arch their back and swim side-to-side to perform a 'keep away' warning display.

Whitetip reef sharks grow up to 2.1 m long and mostly hunt at night. During the day, they may rest in trenches and caves in groups, stacking themselves on top of each other. This shark can sense the faintest of electrical signals, down to as little as one millionth of a volt – the sort of signal given off by the heartbeat of a frightened fish nearby.

Grey reef shark

Whitetip reef sharks

ANGEL SHARKS

These flattish sharks are mostly found on sandy sea beds relatively close to the coast. They look a lot like skates and rays and are also known as monkfish. This is due to the shape of their heads looking like the hood on a monk's cloak.

Angel sharks lie patiently in wait on sandy or muddy sea beds, their top surface blending in with their surroundings. Staying still for long periods means that the angel shark relies on its spiracles to draw in seawater so the shark's blood vessels can absorb oxygen from the water.

When prey such as flatfish, small squid and crustaceans like shrimp get close, the angel shark strikes rapidly. It can lunge and grab prey with its mouth full of needle-shaped teeth in as little as one tenth of a second.

There are at least 22 species of angel shark, with the biggest growing to just over 2 m long. The heaviest weigh around 35 kg.

Their pectoral fins are broad and flat giving the shark a triangular or diamond shape with a long, strong tail.

Japanese angelshark

Sawback angelshark

The shark's eyes are found on the top of their head.

Ocellated angelshark

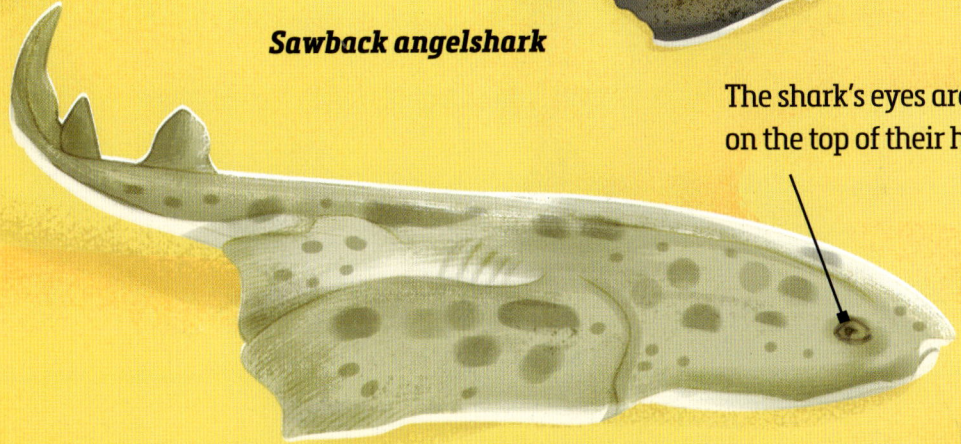

Clouded angelshark

Many coasts have seen increased human activity such as expanding towns, new holiday resorts, increased trawler fishing and high levels of pollution entering the sea.

Living close to the coast has seen angel shark numbers drop by more than half. Some species are now in danger of becoming extinct.

FILTER FEEDERS

The three biggest shark species in the world all eat the smallest possible food. The megamouth shark, whale shark and basking shark are all gentle giants. Instead of hunting and biting, they swim along, mouths open, to filter plankton, small shrimp-like creatures called krill and small fish out of seawater.

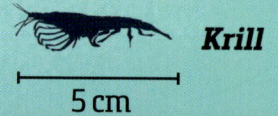

Krill

5 cm

10–12 m

BASKING SHARK

As big as a double decker bus (10-12 m long) and as heavy as an African elephant (5-6 tonnes), this giant shark has an equally giant mouth. It cruises at low speeds with its mouth wide open, letting in 450 tonnes of seawater every hour. Food in the water is trapped by long rows of bristles called gill rakers. The food is swallowed whilst the water leaves the shark via its rows of gill slits.

WHALE SHARK

Even bigger than the basking shark, these massive creatures weigh up to 20 tonnes and can reach an incredible 18 m long although 10-12 m is more common. Their 1.5-m-wide mouths filter out small sea creatures, including fish less than 10 cm long.

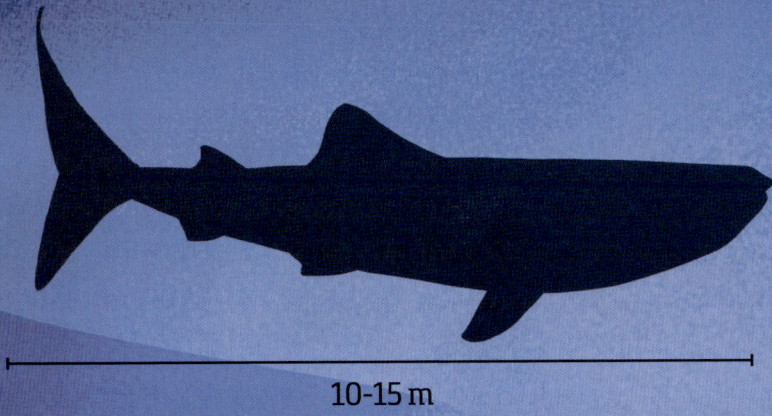

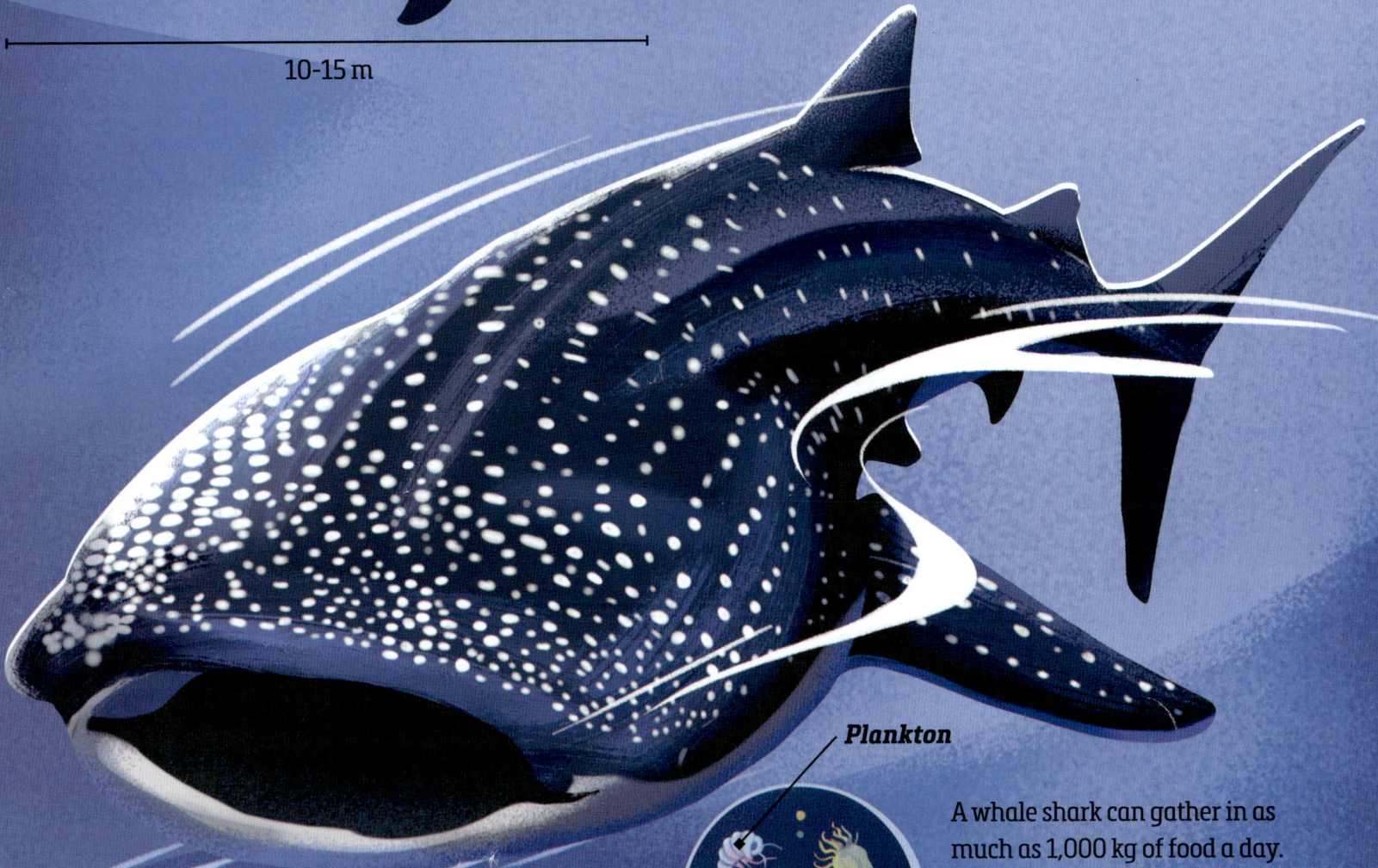

10-15 m

Plankton

A whale shark can gather in as much as 1,000 kg of food a day. They mostly swim in warm waters at shallow depths where plankton is at its most dense, but can dive down more than 1,000 m.

MEGAMOUTH SHARK

Discovered in 1976, the megamouth shark swims at just 1-2 km/h with its 1.4-m-wide mouth open to capture plankton as it moves.

29

CARPET SHARKS

A ROUND 40 SHARKS ARE GROUPED TOGETHER BASED ON THE MOTTLED APPEARANCE OF THEIR BODIES, WHICH LOOK A LITTLE LIKE CARPET PATTERNS. THIS GROUP OF SHARKS ARE INCREDIBLY DIVERSE. THEY RANGE IN SIZE FROM THE GIGANTIC WHALE SHARK (SEE PAGE 29) TO THE BARBELTHROAT CARPET SHARK WHICH GROWS TO LESS THAN 30 CM LONG.

Barbelthroat carpet shark

There are a dozen species of wobbegongs. They often rest during the day, waiting until night when they use their fleshy feelers called barbels, and specially adapted eyesight, to help find prey buried in the sand. Many, like the ornate, spotted and tasselled wobbegongs, live and hunt along the sea bed. Their mottled patterns allow them to blend in on the sea floor where they look like algae and seaweed-covered rocks.

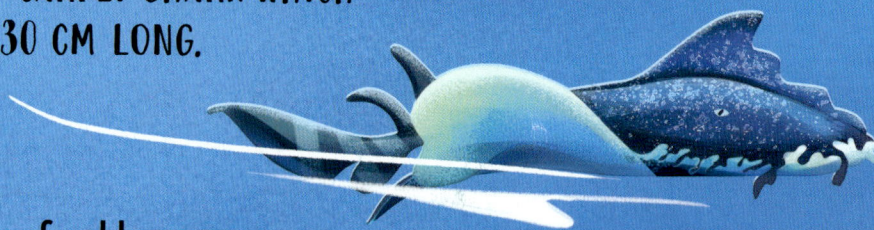

Spotted wobbegong

The tasselled wobbegong (left) has a fringe made of fingers of skin on its head and another fringe on its chin that looks like a beard. It actively hunts at night but whilst resting during the day may lunge at a passing fish which it gathers in its wide mouth.

ZEBRA SHARKS

Adult male and female zebra sharks are around the same size and look very similar. Its their children who look different. Juvenile zebra sharks are a riot of black and white stripes, hence their name.

Adult zebra shark

Juvenile zebra shark

TAKE A WALK

Epaulette sharks are found along the coasts of Australia and New Guinea. These up to 1-m-long sharks have an amazing ability. They can use their broad pectoral and pelvic fins as legs to walk across land between rock pools when the tide is out.

HAMMERHEAD SHARKS

No other creatures on the planet have a head shaped quite like hammerhead sharks. Their wide, mallet-shaped heads, known as *CEPHALOFOILS*, really make them stand out from the crowd.

There are nine species of hammerhead. They range from the 90-cm-long bonnethead shark to the great hammerhead which can grow up to 6.1 m long and weigh as much as 450 kg. Its head can reach 2 m wide. The winghead shark's head is about half as wide as its total body length. Other hammerheads have smaller head widths in proportion to their body. Compared to many other sharks, hammerheads have smaller mouths.

The sharks' mallet-shaped head may act like a hydrofoil under water, giving them extra lift as they move forward and possibly make it easier for them to turn quickly and manoeuvre in water. It also gives them several hunting advantages. With an eye on each end of their head, they can scan a wide area of ocean ahead, above and below in search of potential prey.

Their heads also allow other sense organs, like smell, to work over a wider range. The great hammerhead's ampullae of Lorenzini (see page 19) can detect small electrical signals created by other sea creatures. It allows them to detect stingray and flatfish on the sea bed even if they are well camouflaged. The great hammerhead and scalloped hammerheads sometimes use their head to pin rays to the sea bed when hunting for food.

UNUSUAL SHARKS

Some surprising sharks can be found amongst the more than 500 species which currently exist. Many live at great depths where little sunlight penetrates seawater, so they are not as well-known as other sharks.

GOBLIN SHARK

This scary-looking 3–4 m-long shark has a flabby body and large pointed snout. It drifts through deep seawater. sensing prey from electrical signals. When close enough, it thrusts its jaws a long way forwards like a slingshot. If you could match the goblin shark's abilities, your mouth would extend 18 cm ahead of your nose!

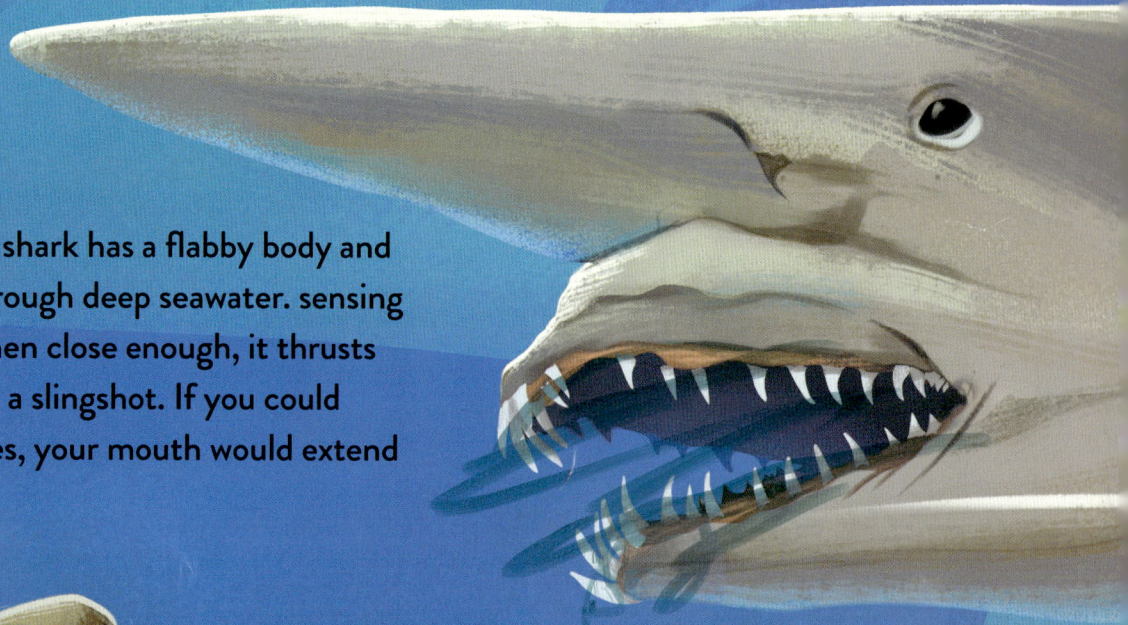

COOKIECUTTER SHARK

The lips of these extraordinary sharks use suction to grip prey far bigger than themselves including seals, whales and large sharks. They then use their lower row of triangular teeth to cut and gouge out a cone-shaped chunk of flesh. When worn down, the entire row of teeth is swallowed and new ones grown as replacements.

FRILLED SHARK

Living at depths of 1,000 metres or more, the frilled shark is a living fossil – the last surviving species of a family of sharks that evolved over 130 million years ago. It possesses an eel-like body and a snake-shaped head inside which are 300 teeth. Each tooth has three prongs like a fork.

GREENEYE SPURDOG

This barely known species of Australian shark spends most of its life in the gloom of the ocean depths, between 280 and 1,400 m below sea level. Mothers give birth to between 4-15 pups after one of the longest pregnancies amongst sharks – as long as three years.

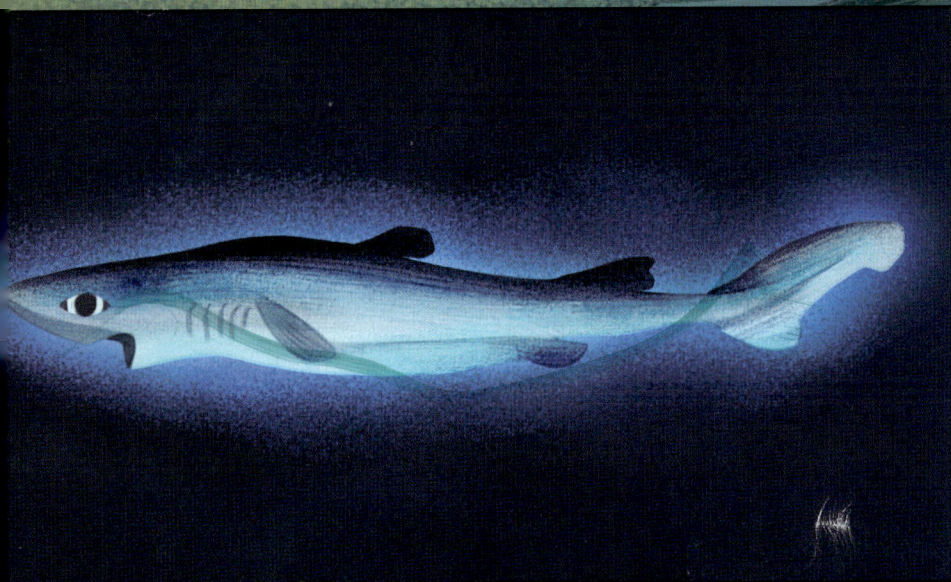

NINJA LANTERNSHARK

Discovered in 2015, this small deep-sea shark has pitch black skin and big, bulbous eyes. Chemicals produced by organs in its body produce light – a process called bioluminescence – which it uses to draw prey nearer to it. Then, it strikes ... quickly.

VIPER DOGFISH

A close relative of the ninja lanternshark, this small, deep sea shark can also produce light. They have teeth like sharp needles and a jaw that can telescope outwards so that the shark can eat prey up to half its own size.

35

THE GREAT WHITE SHARK

THE WORLD'S MOST FAMOUS SHARK SPECIES CAN GROW TO 6-M-LONG AND WEIGH UP TO 1,800 KG. MOST GREAT WHITES ARE A LITTLE SMALLER (3.5-4 M) BUT ARE STILL DEADLY MARINE HUNTERS. THEIR DIET IS VARIED – FROM TUNA AND OTHER BIG, BONY FISH TO DOLPHINS, WHALES, SEALS AND SEA TURTLES.

Sleek and shaped like a torpedo, the great white is partially warm-blooded like the thresher and shortfin mako sharks. This means it can warm its muscles so that they move rapidly. Aided by its powerful tail, great whites can be cruising, then suddenly sprint in short bursts at speeds of 40 km/h or more.

A great white shark's mouth is packed full of 300 triangular teeth some of which grow up to 7.5 cm in size. Powerful jaws give it an exceptionally strong bite. Great whites will often rip out large chunks of flesh, up to 15 kg at a time, but don't chew their food – they swallow the chunks whole.

The great white shark is a highly intelligent hunter, adjusting how it hunts depending on its prey. For surface creatures, it may 'spy hop' at times – poking its head out of the sea to look around. It may also accelerate up and out of the water, breaching at speed to catch seals and sea lions on the surface.

In the water, a great white will use its razor-sharp sense of smell to seek out prey. It will often approach with the Sun at its back. Not only does the sunlight help light up the water ahead so the shark can see more clearly, it may also dazzle its prey.

STUDYING SHARKS

Our knowledge of sharks and their habits and behaviour has grown greatly in the past few decades, but there is still so much more to learn. Scientists use many different technologies to find, follow and examine sharks to learn more about them.

Flying drones are used to track sharks near the surface. Some are equipped with video cameras to film breaching and other behaviour.

Below the water, researchers use underwater robots, travel in submersibles or scuba dive to observe sharks close up.

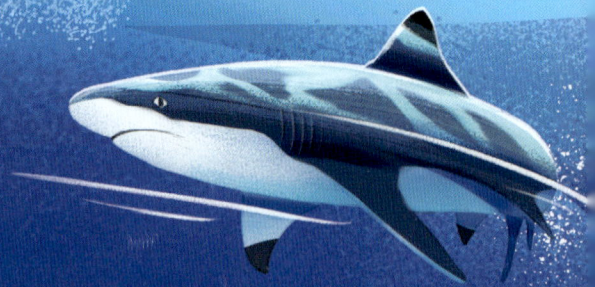

TAGGING

Scientists attach a range of small electronic transmitters, called 'tags', to track sharks. A tag is clipped to a dorsal fin or is surgically implanted under a shark's skin so that it can be tracked for several years at a time. Tags send out radio signals or are fitted with global positioning system (GPS) technology. They allow researchers to track the shark's precise location, how far it travels in a day or season and where its feeding and breeding grounds lie.

Sharks are briefly captured, examined and measured then released back into the water. The data gathered helps build up a better picture of a particular shark population and its health. When a dead shark is found, it is often examined closely to figure out the cause of death and what it had eaten recently.

SCARY SHARKS

SHARKS ARE FORMIDABLE FOES FOR MANY CREATURES IN THE WORLD'S OCEANS BUT HUMANS ARE NOT ON THEIR MENU. SHARKS DO NOT USE THEIR FAMED SUPER SENSES TO TRACK PEOPLE DOWN AS PREY.

Popular films and books have exaggerated the threat from sharks. Less than 40 of the 544 species of shark have ever bitten people. Of these, just a few sharks, such as the great white, tiger and bull sharks, are thought of as repeated attackers whose bite can be deadly.

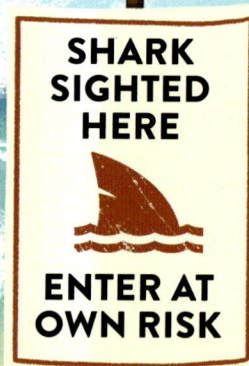

SHARK SIGHTED HERE

ENTER AT OWN RISK

SHARK STATS

According to the International Shark Attack File database, there were 57 unprovoked shark attacks around the world in 2022 and nine deaths from shark bites in total. In the same year, approximately 230,000 people died from drowning. You are 10-15 times more likely to be killed by a falling coconut than a shark.

Most shark bites come from curiosity or a scared shark trying to defend itself. Some have occurred when bottom-dwelling sharks, such as wobbegongs, lying still on the sea bed are stepped on by humans. Others have come when mostly young sharks are hungry and mistake a flash of a coloured surfboard or swimwear for a tasty fish or squid. These are accidents rather than a shark stalking and attacking humans for food.

STAY SAFE

Never enter the sea alone and only in designated bathing areas, usually marked by flags. Follow any signals displayed or sounded by lifeguards. Many sharks are at their most hungry and ready to feed around dawn and dusk. Coastal sharks tend to be drawn to sandbars, river mouths and piers where there is often a rich concentration of plankton, fish and other marine creatures. Avoid these areas and where the water is murky.

SHARK SURVIVOR

Paul de Gelder was an Australian military diver who was surprised by a bull shark which took off his right leg and lower arm with one bite in 2009. Paul has since become a passionate advocate for protecting sharks and conserving their ocean environment. "Most people will never see a shark in their life," he said in a 2022 interview, "so their views come from news reports, childhood fears and works of fiction. Every shark is different and amazing. They're all spectacular in their own way."

41

LIVING WITH SHARKS

SOME PEOPLE HUNT SHARKS, FEARING THEY AFFECT THEIR LOCAL LIVELIHOOD FROM FISHING OR TOURISM, OR TO MAKE MONEY FROM SELLING THE SHARK'S SKIN, TEETH AND OTHER BODY PARTS. MANY COASTAL COMMUNITIES, HOWEVER, TRY TO LIVE IN HARMONY WITH SHARKS IN THE WATERS NEARBY.

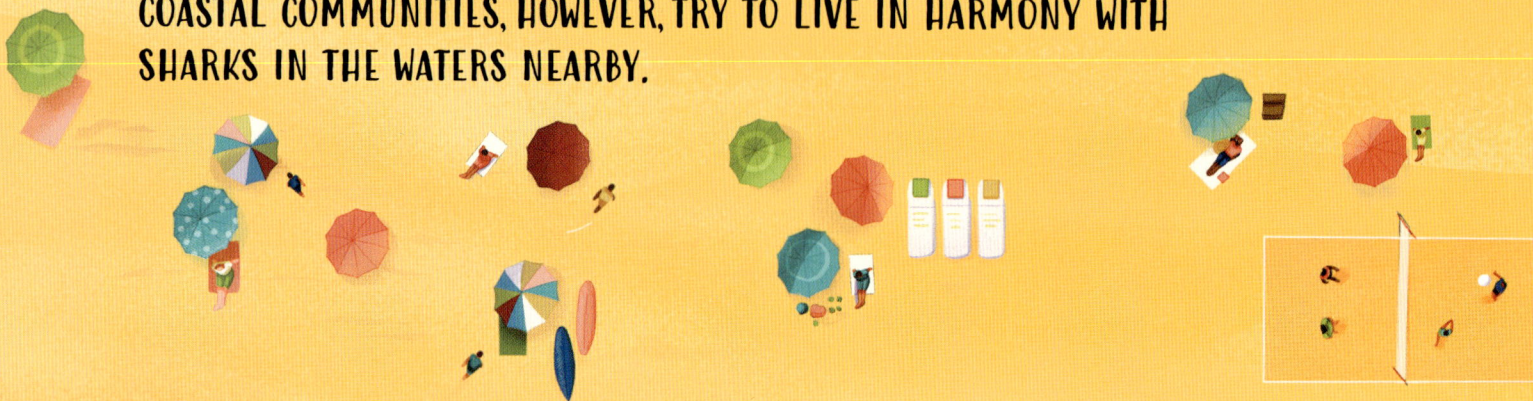

To safeguard bathers and beaches, some places erect physical barriers such as netting or giant floating fishing hooks called 'drumlines' in the shallows by a beach. These may repel sharks but they often entangle and kill them as well as turtles, rays and dolphins. Electronic deterrents are less harmful. These send out electrical signals that disrupt the shark's electrical detectors, causing the shark to swim away.

Some beaches and bays feature lifeguards trained to spot the presence of dangerous sharks. Robot drones, like Australia's Little Ripper, can fly above the water and use their cameras to identify shark species and send out an alert if any dangerous sharks are close by.

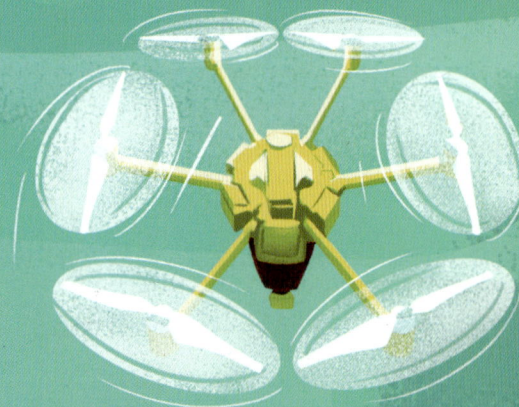

Sharks can be worth more alive than dead. Shark-rich seas in some places attract tourists keen to see these incredible creatures in the wild. Some people swim alongside peaceful whale sharks or stand inside a secure shark cage lowered into the water so they get up close to sharks. Shark-spotting tours from land, on ships or underwater in diving tours can boost the local economy if they are performed responsibly.

SAVE THE SHARK

SHARKS ARE FASCINATING CREATURES BUT MANY ARE UNDER TERRIBLE THREAT. MORE THAN ONE-THIRD OF ALL SHARK AND RAY SPECIES ARE IN DANGER OF EXTINCTION THROUGH THREATS AS VARIED AS SPORTS FISHING AND CULLING BY COASTAL COMMUNITIES.

The number one threat to sharks is the growing demand for shark meat, shark fins and shark liver oil. Over 100 million sharks are killed every year, most for food. Overfishing is leading to shark populations dwindling fast. Compared to many fish, sharks take a long time to mature and reproduce.

The numbers of great hammerhead sharks have dropped more than 80 per cent in the past 70 years.

Sharks' habitats are being increasingly harmed by pollution – from oil and chemical spills to the growing amounts of waste plastics in water. Changes in ocean temperature and acidity, caused by climate change, are having a devastating effect. These changes are damaging coral reefs and the populations of fish, squid and other creatures sharks rely on for food.

Thousands of sharks are killed unintentionally each year, trapped in fishing nets designed to catch other creatures.

It's not all bad news. Conservationists and campaigners have had some success. A handful of countries have banned the sale of some shark products, whilst some species are protected from overfishing.

A number of shark sanctuaries have been set up in the Indian and Pacific Oceans as well as the Caribbean Sea. In these areas, shark fishing is banned, giving these magnificent creatures precious time to increase their numbers.

45

GLOSSARY

Barbel Fleshy whiskers near some sharks' mouths that help sharks detect food.

Bioluminescence Light produced by living things, including some sharks.

Cartilage Firm, strong but flexible tissue which forms the skeleton of sharks.

Climate change A change in the usual weather for an area over a long period of time.

Crustaceans A group of creatures with hard shells and many legs, including crabs, lobsters and shrimp.

Cull Killing wild animals to reduce their numbers.

Cartilage Firm, strong but flexible tissue which forms the skeleton of sharks.

Ecosystem An area that contains interacting animals and plants and the surroundings they exist in.

Embryo An animal that is developing either in an egg or its mother's womb.

Gills The breathing organs of sharks and fish.

Hydrofoil A wing, which when it travels through water, provides lift, causing objects to rise.

Lateral line A row of sense organs found down the side of a shark's body that detect movement in the water.

Litter The name given to a collection of live baby sharks.

Pectoral fins A pair of fins found towards the front of a shark.

Plankton Microscopic plant or animal life found in vast numbers in the ocean.

Prehistoric The time before there was written or recorded history – stretching from approximately 6,000 years or so ago back millions of years.

School A large group of fish that swim closely together.

Spiracles Openings in a shark's body that let in seawater to help supply oxygen to a shark's blood.

Tendril A thin, slender, cord-like growth.

Venomous A creature or body part which produces harmful substances that can injure or kill other creatures.

FURTHER INFORMATION

Books

Blue Worlds series (The Pacific Oceans/The Southern Ocean/The Arctic Ocean/The Atlantic Ocean/The Indian Ocean/Seas, Gulfs and Bays) – Anita Ganeri (Wayland, 2022)

If Sharks Disappeared – Lily Williams (Franklin Watts, 2017)

Interview with a Shark – Andy Seed (Welbeck, 2018)

Life at Extremes: Under the Sea – Josy Bloggs (Franklin Watts, 2023)

Predator versus Prey: How Sharks and Other Fish Attack – Tim Harris (Wayland, 2020)

Sharks: Get Up Close to Nature's Fiercest Predators – Ben Hubbard (Welbeck, 2016)

Websites

www.marineconservation.org.au/save-our-sharks/

The Marine Conservation Organisation is dedicated to protecting ocean wildlife. This webpage shows why sharks are important and how we can help to save them.

www.sharktrust.org/pages/category/discover-sharks

The Shark Trust is dedicated to helping conserve sharks and this website contains fact files and videos on many shark species.

www.sharks.org/species

View the great variety of sharks with these webpages of illustrations of sharks. Click on a picture to call up key data about a particular shark.

www.sharksider.com/

A fun website with facts and images created by shark-loving divers and surfers.

www.floridamuseum.ufl.edu/shark-attacks/reduce-risk/quick-tips/

A series of tips and videos on how to avoid trouble with sharks.

INDEX